T0004927

KNOCK-KNOCK ROCKS!

MORE THAN 444 JOKES FOR KIDS!

LOL-
APALOOZA
JOKES

An Imprint of Thomas Nelson

Published in Nashville, Tennessee, by Tommy Nelson. Tommy Nelson
is an imprint of Thomas Nelson. Thomas Nelson is a registered
trademark of HarperCollins Christian Publishing, Inc.

Tommy Nelson titles may be purchased in bulk for educational,
business, fund-raising, or sales promotional use. For information,
please e-mail SpecialMarkets@ThomasNelson.com.

Jokes provided by Tommy Marshall.

Library of Congress Cataloging-in-Publication Data

Title: LOL-apalooza : more than 444 jokes for kids.
Description: Nashville, Tennessee : Tommy Nelson, [2019] | Audience: Ages
  6-10. |
Identifiers: LCCN 2019005674 (print) | LCCN 2019011145 (ebook) | ISBN
  9781400216628 (ebook) | ISBN 9781400214389 | ISBN
  9781400214389(softcover :alk. paper)
Subjects: LCSH: Wit and humor, Juvenile.
Classification: LCC PN6166 (ebook) | LCC PN6166 .L64 2019 (print) | DDC
  818/.60208--dc23
LC record available at https://lccn.loc.gov/2019005674

Printed in the United States of America

19 20 21 22 LSC 6 5 4 3 2 1

Mfr: LSC / Crawfordsville, IN / July 2019 / PO #9531486

Contents

Jokes, Jokes, and More Jokes

Q: What was Noah's favorite fruit?

A: Pears.

Q: What do Kermit the Frog and Winnie the Pooh have in common?

A: Their middle names.

Q: What is something cats have that no other animal has?

A: Kittens!

Q: Why did King Arthur have a round table?

A: So he couldn't be cornered.

Q: Why is a car like an elephant?

A: They both have trunks.

Q: What card game do porcupines like the most?

A: Poker.

Q: What snack food do computers like the most?

A: Chips.

Q: What do bad stories and broken pencils have in common?

A: Neither one has a point.

Q: What meal do astronauts like the most?

A: Launch.

Q: What food do snowmen like the most?

A: Ice Krispie treats.

Q: What color do kittens like the most?

A: PURRRRRple.

Q: What dessert do kittens like the most?

A: Mice cream.

Q: Why is it usually windy in a soccer stadium?

A: It is full of fans.

Q: What type of precipitation do queens like the most?

A: Reign!

Q: What type of precipitation do kings like the most?

A: Hail!

I decided to quit my job as a baker.

Really? Why?

I wasn't making enough dough.

....

Any idea what happened
to the lightning?

No. Why?

Oh, never mind.
It just struck me!

Q: What dessert do math teachers like the most?

A: Pi.

Q: What amusement park ride do watches like the most?

A: A merry-go-round.

Q: What letter do pirates like the most?

A: You think it's the RRRR! But it's really the C!

Q: How many different cars did the apostles drive?

A: They were actually all in one Accord.

Q: When does a car stop being a car?

A: When it turns into a garage.

Q: What game do tornadoes love to play?

A: Twister!

Q: What do you call a dog that sneezes a lot?

A: ACHOOwawa!

Q: Where do bunnies go when they get married?

A: On their bunnymoon!

Q: Was Benjamin Franklin happy when he discovered electricity?

A: No, he was shocked!

Q: When is it a good idea to bring a pet skunk to school?

A: When it is show-and-smell!

Q: What is black and white and red all over?

A: A newspaper.

Q: What is black and white and red all over?

A: A tomato wearing a tuxedo.

Q: What is black and white and flies when you kick it?

A: A soccer ball.

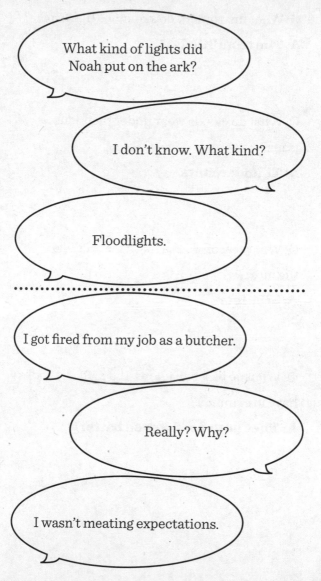

What kind of lights did Noah put on the ark?

I don't know. What kind?

Floodlights.

I got fired from my job as a butcher.

Really? Why?

I wasn't meating expectations.

9

Q: What instrument do skeletons like to play?

A: The tromBONE.

Q: What do clouds wear under their blue jeans?

A: Thunderpants.

Q: What season does a math teacher like the most?

A: SUMmer.

Q: What do baseball teams and pancake cooks have in common?

A: They both need a good batter!

Q: Why did the fitness nut love light-years?

A: Because they're the same as regular years but with fewer calories.

Q: Why are ducks good at math?

A: They have their own QUACKulators!

Q: When is a green textbook not a green textbook?

A: When it is read!

Q: What did the bear call the hiker in a sleeping bag?

A: A burrito.

Q: What key on the keyboard do astronauts like the most?

A: **The space bar!**

Q: Who pays for dinner when a duck and a cow go on a date?

A: **The duck! (She has the bill!)**

Q: What do grass and an elephant have in common?

A: **They're both green ... except for the elephant.**

Q: What dessert do basketball players love the most?

A: **Cookies! (Because they can dunk them!)**

Q: What school subject do snakes like the most?

A: HISStory.

Q: Why did the birds fly south for the winter?

A: The drive was going to take too long.

Q: What drink do trees like the most?

A: Root beer.

Q: What does the cow say every December 25th?

A: MOO-ey Christmas!

Q: Why was the football coach hitting the soda machine?

A: He wanted his quarter back.

Q: Why did Tommy wear stilts to class?

A: He wanted to be in high school.

Q: Who did the monster bring to the dance?

A: His GHOULfriend.

Q: Why didn't the bald eagles make any plans?

A: They liked to wing it.

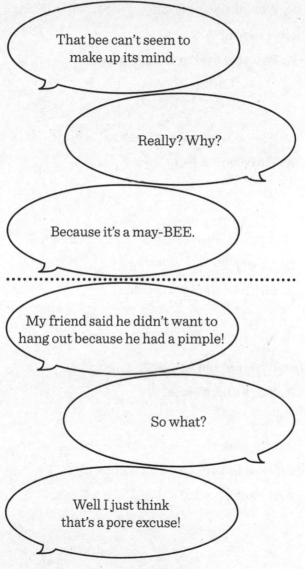

15

Q: What is the first thing you do when teaching elves to read?

A: You start with the elf-a-bet.

Q: What did the elephant say to his bride?

A: I love you a ton.

Q: Why did the music teacher get picked first for baseball?

A: She had perfect pitch.

Q: What did the farmer give his wife?

A: Hogs and kisses.

Q: What is salty, crunchy, and can fly?

A: A rocket chip!

Q: What do false teeth and stars have in common?

A: They both come out at night.

Q: Why was the fish so smart?

A: It spent its whole life in a school.

Q: Why is the frog always in a good mood?

A: It eats whatever bugs it.

Q: What time of day did God create Adam?

A: A little before EVE-ning.

Q: What do history teachers talk about at the high school reunion?

A: The good old days.

Q: What do bananas and gymnasts have in common?

A: They can both do the splits.

Q: What did George Washington's dad say after he cut down the cherry tree?

A: Nothing. He was stumped!

Q: What is green when it flies through the air but red when it hits the ground?

A: A watermelon.

Q: Why are windows no good at poker?

A: You can see right through them.

Q: Why did Humpty Dumpty sit on the wall?

A: He thought it was an EGGSellent idea.

Q: Why did Humpty Dumpty have a great fall?

A: He really enjoyed watching the leaves change color.

Q: Why did Humpty Dumpty get ignored by the king's men?

A. They thought he was cracked!

Q: Did you hear the joke about the broken pencil?

A: Aaah, never mind. It was pointless.

Q: Did you hear what happened at the laundromat yesterday?

A: A half-dozen clothespins held up a bunch of shirts!

Q: Did you hear about the angry leprechaun?

A: He was short-tempered!

Q: Did you hear the burrito singing?

A: Actually, it was more of a wrap.

Q: Did you hear about the kidnapping?

A: His mom woke him up.

Q: Did you hear about the basketball player who broke her left arm?

A: She's all right now.

Q: Did you hear about the fireworks party?

A: It was a bang-up good time!

Q: Why did the kid eat his test?

A: The teacher said it was a piece of cake!

Q: Why did the kid take all year to finish a book?

A: He wasn't very hungry.

Q: Why did the boy's grades drop after the holidays?

A: Because everything was marked down!

Q: Why did the girl throw the clock out the window?

A: She wanted to see time fly!

Q: What do you call it when a cat wins a dog show?

A: A Cat-has-trophy.

Q: Did you know whales can squirt out ink when they're scared?

A: Naaah, just squidding!

Q: How did the chef know the salmon was done?

A: He heard the smoked detector!

Q: What do mathematicians eat on Halloween?

A: Pumpkin pi.

Q: What is the most popular side item on Halloween?

A: French frights!

Q: How did the composer get the crowd to move?

A: He just kept saying, "Bach! Bach!"

Q: What did the lawyer wear to court?

A: A lawsuit.

Q: Why did the nose come home from school crying?

A: He was picked on all day!

Q: What did the plate say to the serving dish?

A: Hey, dinner's on me!

Q: Why were the kids all tired on April Fool's Day?

A: They had just finished a 31-day March!

Q: Did Renoir love to paint?

A: No, he just did it for the Monet!

Q: What did the sea monster eat for lunch?

A: Fish and ships.

Q: Why did the shoemakers all go to heaven?

A: They had great soles!

Q: What did the skeleton chef say to her guests?

A: Bone appétit!

Q: What did the snowmen do all weekend?

A: Just chill.

Q: What did the snowmen eat for breakfast?

A: Frosted Flakes.

Q: What did the snowmen do for the holidays?

A: Played with the snow angels.

Q: What do snowmen call their kids?

A: CHILLdren.

Q: What do snowmen wear on their heads?

A: Ice caps.

Q: What flower do squirrels like the most?

A: Forget-me-nuts.

Q: What is smarter than a talking parrot?

A: A spelling bee!

Q: What do dinosaurs smell like?

A: Ex-stinked.

Q: Why was the fish at the bottom of the ocean?

A: It dropped out of school!

Q: What is the difference between a guitar and a fish?

A: You can't tuna fish.

Who was the best comedian in the Bible?

I don't know. Who?

Samson. He brought the house down.

• •

I'm so fed up with sticky playing cards!

Really? Why?

I just find them really hard to deal with!

Q: Why was the little strawberry worried?

A: His mom was in a jam!

Q: What made the stoplight blush?

A: People were watching it change.

Q: Why did the belt get arrested?

A: It was holding up a pair of pants.

Q: Why was the math book worn down?

A: It was full of problems.

Q: Why was the hungry clock always late?

A: It kept going back for seconds.

Q: How did the computer get wet?

A: It left a window open!

Q: Why was the clown so sad?

A: She broke her funny bone.

Q: Why was the baseball player in trouble with his friends?

A: He stole two bases and then went home.

Q: Why was the band mad at the baseball player?

A: For stealing a bass!

Q: What part of the orchestra did the baseball player conduct?

A: He ran the basses.

Q: Why was the janitor late for work?

A: He overSWEPT.

Q: How did the janitor do in the play?

A: He swept them away!

Q: What kind of gestures do janitors make?

A: Sweeping!

Q: Why did the kid keep checking his dad's pockets for food?

A: His dad said, "Dinner is on me!"

Q: Why were the scientists all wet?

A: They had been brainstorming.

Q: Why did the pelican get mad leaving the restaurant?

A: He had a big bill!

Q: Why did the Italian man want to kiss the angle?

A: He-a thought it was a-cute.

Q: Why was the angle never right?

A: Because it was obtuse!

Q: Why did the kid keep staring at his orange juice?

A: The box said concentrate!

Q: Why was the soup so expensive?

A: It had 24 carrots!

Q: What kind of dog loves fire?

A: A hotdog.

Q: Why was the pharaoh crying?

A: He wanted his mummy.

Q: Why wouldn't they let the turkey into
the buffet?

A: Because he would gobble it up.

Q: How did the vegetable farmers get married?

A: With 14 carrot rings!

Q: Why is Atlas the most wanted thief
in history?

A: Because he held up the entire world.

Q: How did they divide up Rome?

A: With a pair of Caesars.

Q: Why does the pharaoh keep bragging?

A: He sphinx he's the best.

Q: Why were the married hikers freaked out?

A: They were two in-tents.

Q: What made the fish blush?

A: It could see the lake's bottom.

Q: Why was the chef so proud of her cucumber?

A: She knew it would one day be a big dill.

Q: Why did the chef put the pickle on the top shelf?

A: It was a really big dill.

Q: What did the tomato say to the little pickle?

A: You're no big dill!

Q: What made the lettuce blush?

A: It could see the salad dressing.

Q: What do vegetables say in church?

A: Lettuce pray.

Q: Why did the cookie take its medicine?

A: It felt crumby.

Q: Why did the antique dealer sell her cookies cheap?

A: They had too many chips.

Q: Why did the sick monkey climb into the fridge?

A: It wanted to feel butter.

Q: Why did the toilet paper roll down the hill?

A: To get to the bottom.

Q: What was Eve's favorite food?

A: Ribs.

Q: Why did the golfer wear two pairs of pants?

A: He thought he was going to get a hole in one.

Q: Why did the monkey bars move across the playground?

A: They were trying to get to the other slide.

Q: Why did the gorilla go to the playground when he turned 21?

A: For the monkey bars.

Q: Why did Jack bring a ladder to school?

A: He was having trouble getting into high school.

Q: Why did the orange not get a date?

A: It wasn't a-PEEL-ing.

Q: Why did the teddy bear not want any ice cream?

A: Because it was stuffed.

Q: Why did the banana stop taking its medicine?

A: It started peeling better.

Q: How do you send an innocent picture to jail?

A: You frame it!

Q: Why did the kid put her guitar in the snow?

A: She likes cool tunes.

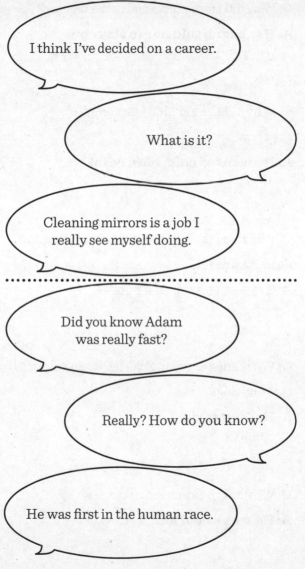

Q: Why did the boxer stand in the freezer?

A: Her coach told her to stay cool.

Q: Why did the kid hide his money in the snow?

A: He wanted cold, hard cash!

Q: What do you do when it is raining cats and dogs outside?

A: Try not to step in a poodle.

Q: What does everyone like less than raining cats and dogs?

A: Hailing taxis!

Q: Why did the kid need a sweater?

A: He was a cool kid.

Q: What kind of horse chews with its mouth closed?

A: One with good stable manners.

Q: Why did the pony get in trouble?

A: It wouldn't stop horsing around.

Q: Why was the horse kicked out of the poker game?

A: He wouldn't pony up what he owed.

Q: Why were the ponies kicked out of the theater?

A: Too much horseplay.

Q: Why did the robber steal so much soap?

A: So he could make a clean getaway.

Q: Why did the kid keep running around his bed?

A: He was trying to catch up on sleep.

Q: Why did the kid keep running around his textbook?

A: He was trying to catch up on homework.

Q: Why did the teacher wear sunglasses in school?

A: Her students were too bright.

Q: Why did the cyclops quit teaching school?

A: He only had one pupil.

Q: How did the hairdresser get done first?

A: **With a short cut.**

Q: Why did Dad put lipstick on his forehead?

A: **Mom told him to make up his mind.**

Q: Why did Dad put ice on his forehead?

A: **Mom told him to chill out.**

Q: Why did Dad put a banana on his head?

A: **Mom told him he should try to look more a-PEEL-ing.**

Q: Why did the lettuce beat the tomato in a race?

A: Because it was a head.

Q: Why did the computer take its medicine?

A: Because it had a virus.

Q: Why did the chickadee go to the doctor?

A: For a TWEETment.

Q: How do beavers surf the web?

A: They just log on.

Q: Why did the beaver eat the light bulb?

A: It wanted a light snack.

Q: Why did the ice cream wiggle?

A: It wanted to see the milkshake.

Q: Why did the ice scream?

A: It thought it saw the milk shake.

Q: Why did the kids all shout at their snow cones?

A: To make the ice scream.

Q: Why did the traffic light turn red?

A: It was changing right in the middle of the street.

Q: Why did the baseball player ask for some rope?

A: She wanted to tie the score.

Q: Why do plants go to the dentist?

A: For root canals.

Q: Why did Sam do his homework on a plane?

A: He wanted a higher education.

Q: How did the farmer fix his clothes?

A: With cabbage patches.

Q: Why did the orange juice worker get fired?

A: He wasn't concentrating.

Q: Why did the teacher throw an exam in the lake?

A: To test the waters.

Q: Why did the teacher use a window instead of a chalkboard?

A: He wanted the lesson to be very clear.

Q: Why did the teacher put watches on all the desk chairs?

A: She wanted all her students in class on time.

Q: Why did the bubblegum burst?

A: Because the lolly popped.

Q: Why did the can explode?

A: Because the soda popped.

Q: Why did the computer scream?

A: It saw a mouse.

Q: Why did the sun want to go to school?

A: It wanted to feel brighter.

Q: Why did the cantaloupe jump into the lake?

A: It wanted to be a watermelon.

Q: Why did the watermelons refuse to get married?

A: They were told they can't elope.

Q: Why did the chemist put a big knocker on her lab door?

A: She wanted to win the No Bell Prize!

Q: Why did the singer join the sailors?

A: So he could hit the high Cs.

Q: Why didn't the fours need lunch?

A: They already eight.

Q: Why was six afraid of seven?

A: Because seven eight nine.

Q: How do you know it is a dad joke?

A: When it becomes apparent.

Q: How does the apostle Paul make coffee?

A: Hebrews it.

Q: Why can't you play poker in the jungle?

A: Too many cheetahs.

Q: How do you make nachos dance?

A: Put on the salsa.

Q: Why did the tiger eat the tightrope walker?

A: It liked a balanced diet.

Q: Why did the opera singer climb the ladder?

A: To hit the high notes.

Q: Why did the right angle turn off the heat?

A: Because it was already 90 degrees.

Q: Why did the bucket's mom give him medicine?

A: He looked pail.

Q: Why did the rope take some medicine?

A: Its stomach was in knots.

Q: Why did the kids put Grandma's rocking chair on their skateboard?

A: So she could rock and roll.

Q: Why did the dalmatian think she needed medicine?

A: She kept seeing spots.

Q: Why did the dalmatian get fired?

A: She had a spotty work record.

Q: Why didn't the pine tree order its ice cream in a dish?

A: It already had a cone.

Q: Why did the T. rex need a bandage?

A: It had a dino sore.

Q: What makes a dinosaur?

A: Kick it in the shins.

Q: How do you keep a banana from peeling?

A: Lots of sunscreen. And maybe a hat?

Q: Why did the park ranger kick the cat out of the park?

A: Because of its litter.

Q: Why did the frankfurter turn on the heat?

A: It was a chili dog.

Q: Why did the frankfurter turn on the air conditioning?

A: It was a hot dog.

Q: What do you tell a frankfurter posing for pictures?

A: Say cheese, dawg!

Q: Why did the frankfurter tell all of these bad jokes?

A: It was a corn dog.

Q: Why did the cat sit on the keyboard?

A: It was watching the mouse.

Q: Why did the dog keep getting splinters in his tongue?

A: He wouldn't stop eating table scraps.

Q: Why did the dog keep begging for food?

A: Because things were RUFF.

Q: Did you hear the joke about the balloon?

A: Aaah, never mind. It was over your head.

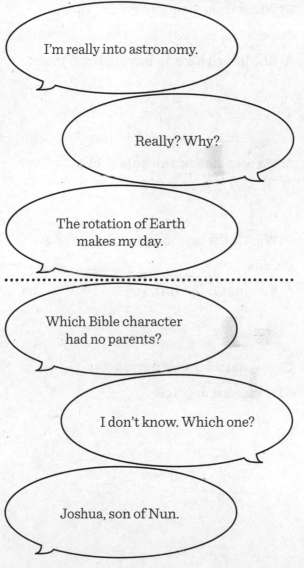

I'm really into astronomy.

Really? Why?

The rotation of Earth makes my day.

Which Bible character had no parents?

I don't know. Which one?

Joshua, son of Nun.

Q: Why did my mom give my dad a dog and a watch?

A: She heard he was having a ruff time.

Q: Why did the baker quit the bagel business?

A: He was sick of the hole thing.

Q: What is the best way to begin studying the Bible?

A: You just Luke into it.

Q: Why did the grapefruit stop?

A: It ran out of juice.

Q: What does a bee do when he finds his honey?

A: He asks her to marry him!

Q: Why did the bee keep swimming?

A: She was in the middle of A C.

Q: Why did the snake quit the movie business?

A: There were no parts he could really sink his teeth into.

Q: Why did the astronaut throw cold cuts on an asteroid?

A: He preferred it a little meteor.

Q: Why was the grandfather clock kicked out of school?

A: For tocking too much.

Q: Why did the students think their teacher was a ghost?

A: She went through things over and over!

Q: Why did the students steal all the chairs?

A: The teacher told them to take a seat.

Q: Who brings toilet paper to a celebration?

A: A party pooper!

Q: Why did the farmer steamroll his fields?

A: He was making mashed potatoes.

Q: Why did the farmer steamroll his fields?

A: He wanted to grow squash.

Q: How do you mail a balloon?

A: Burst Class.

Q: How do you mail a stopwatch?

A: Second Class.

Q: How do you mail a turkey?

A: Bird Class.

Q: How did the telephone propose to his girlfriend?

A: He gave her a ring.

Q: What do you call a phone on a lanyard?

A: Ring around the collar.

Q: What do you hear when the phone goes off at a baseball field?

A: A diamond ring.

Q: How did the egg avoid getting tackled?

A: It scrambled.

Q: Why did the paintbrush need medicine?

A: It had a stroke.

Q: How did Vikings communicate?

A: Through Norse code.

Q: How did the pearl get to the hospital?

A: In a clam-bulance.

Q: Why did the detective quiz the shellfish?

A: He thought something looked fishy.

Q: How did the shellfish frustrate the detective?

A: They all clammed up.

Q: Who did the shellfish use for protection?

A: The mussels.

Q: Why did the bread get fired?

A: For loafing around.

Q: Why couldn't the cookie dough find investors?

A: His ideas were half-baked.

Q: Why did the nut go out with a prune?

A: Because it couldn't find a date.

Q: What is an easy way to catch a squirrel?

A: Climb a tree and act like a nut.

Q: What is wrong with the food squirrels eat?

A: They're nuts!

Q: What did the squirrel think of her dinner?

A: That it was nutty.

Q: Why did the squirrel love all the college kids?

A: He thought they were nuts!

Q: If Jesus came down to Earth today, what kind of car would he drive?

A: Christ-ler.

Q: What is the weather like in the Mexican restaurant?

A: Chili today and hot tamale.

Q: What part of the eye works the hardest?

A: The pupil.

Q: What is the world's tallest building?

A: The library—it has the most stories!

Q: What is the difference between your gym teacher and a train?

A: One says, "Spit out your gum!" and the other says, "Chew! Chew!"

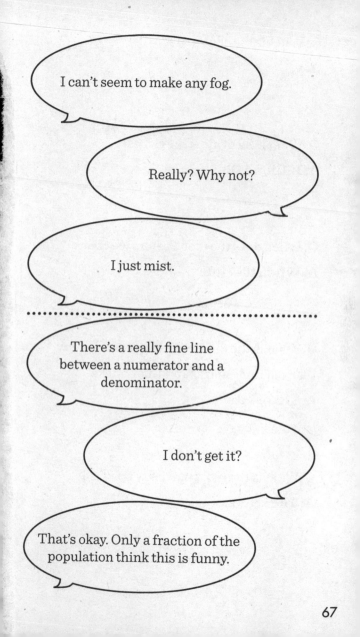

I can't seem to make any fog.

Really? Why not?

I just mist.

There's a really fine line between a numerator and a denominator.

I don't get it?

That's okay. Only a fraction of the population think this is funny.

Q: What is the center of gravity?

A: v.

Q: What kind of air is the richest?

A: BillionAIRe.

Q: When does the moon refuse ice cream?

A: When it is full.

Q: What is the difference between a twenty-year-old dime and a brand-new nickel?

A: Five cents.

Q: What is the most musical part of a fish?

A: The scales.

Q: What is the best musical instrument ever?

A: A broken drum. You can't beat it!

Q: What question can you never answer truthfully?

A: Are you asleep?

Q: Why don't you watch movies with your cat?

A: Because it keeps hitting paws!

Q: What do a cloned cat and a cheating cat have in common?

A: One is a cat copy and the other is a copy cat.

Q: What is bigger than you but weighs nothing?

A: Your shadow (sometimes).

Q: Why do whales drink orange juice?

A: For the vitamin sea.

Q: What did the janitor order to his
hotel room?

A: Broom service.

Q: Why did the two goldfish in the tank stay
totally still?

A: Neither one knew how to drive it.

Q: What did the hip-hop pharaoh ask Noah?

A: **"Who let the frogs out? Who? Who? Who? Who?"**

Q: What kind of pants did Noah wear?

A: **Floods.**

Q: How many disciples did it take to change the light bulb?

A: **NONE—they could already see the light.**

Q: What is the title of a fairy-tale movie with eight characters?

A: *Snow White and the Seven Dwarfs.*

Q: Why was the address book jealous of the calendar?

A: The calendar had all the dates.

Q: How do you stop seven from being odd?

A: Take away the s—now it's even.

Q: Why did the spider never go out to play a lot of sports?

A: Because it was always on the web.

Q: Why did the spider's girlfriend break up with him?

A: He wouldn't get off the web.

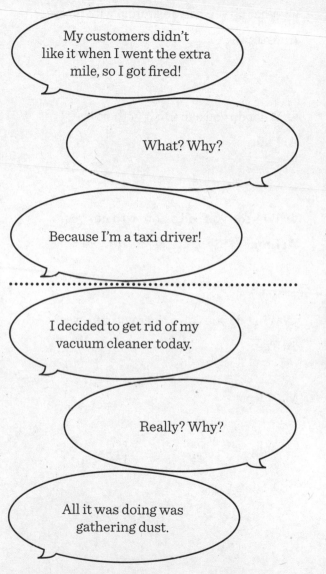

Q: What do you call an animal with no eyes?

A: Anmal.

Q: What do you call a fish with no eyes?

A: Fsh.

Q: What do you call a lion with no eyes?

A: Lon.

Q: What do you call a tiger with no eyes?

A: Tger.

Q: What do you call a giraffe with no eyes?

A: Graffe.

Q: What do you call a pig with no eyes?

A: Pg.

Q: What do you call a bird with no eyes?

A: Brd … hmm … sounds the same.

Q: Fine, what do you call a deer with
no eyes?

A: No eye deer!

Q: One last one—what do you call an animal
with ten eyes?

A: An aniiiiiiiiiimal!

Q: How do you know which side of a worm is the head?

A: Ask it a question and see where it answers from.

Q: What do you call a classroom full of rabbits backing up?

A: A receding hare line.

Q: What do you call a rabbit invention?

A: A HAREbrained idea.

Q: Did the rabbits win the relay race?

A: Yep. By a hare.

Q: What do you call a cow with no legs?

A: Ground beef.

Q: What do you call a dog with no legs?

A: Doesn't matter. It won't come.

Q: What do you call a dog with no legs at your front door?

A: Matt.

Q: What do you call a dog with no legs swimming in your pool?

A: Bob.

Q: What do you call a fly with no wings?

A: A walk.

Q: What do I call my cheese?

A: Nacho cheese!

Q: What do you call a bull when it is fast asleep?

A: A bulldozer.

Q: What do you need when you drop a lemon off a balcony?

A: Lemon aid.

Q: What do you call a boomerang that doesn't come back?

A: A stick.

Q: What do you do when you're swallowed by a whale?

A: Start running and don't stop until you're all pooped out.

Q: What do you call a whole bunch of giraffes trying to fit between two trees?

A: A giraffic jam!

Q: What do you call a kid with a rubber toe?

A: Roberto.

Q: Why couldn't the duck sell its windows?

A: They were all quacked.

Q: What do you get when you combine a snake and a snowman?

A: Frost bite.

Q: What do you call a duck that gets straight As?

A: A wise quacker.

Q: Why shouldn't you go to a duck doctor?

A: Most of them are quacks.

Q: What do you call guard ducks on a farm?

A: Animal quackers.

Q: What's the best way to talk to a giant?

A: With really big words.

Q: Why is it hard to read a book written by a giant?

A: It is full of BIG words.

Q: What do you call two birds in love?

A: Tweethearts.

Q: Why did the amazing chef have to close his restaurant on Mars?

A: The food was great, but the atmosphere was terrible!

Q: What kind of footwear do you make with bananas?

A: Slippers.

Q: What do you call a plate of fake spaghetti?

A: Impasta.

Q: How do you fix a broken pumpkin?

A: With a pumpkin patch.

Q: Why did the kids laugh at the mountain?

A: Because it was HILLarious!

Q: What do you call a snowman on the beach?

A: A puddle.

Q: What do you call a bear in a rainstorm?

A: A drizzly bear.

Q: What kind of cow joins a band?

A: A MOOsician.

Q: Why did the musician cancel her concert?

A: She decided it wasn't worth the treble.

Q: What do you usually break before using it?

A: An egg.

Q: What do you get when you combine a Christmas tree with an apple?

A: A pine-apple.

Q: What is in December but no other month?

A: D.

Q: What do you call an elephant in a phone booth?

A: A stuck elephant.

Q: Why did the Florida puppy pitch left-handed?

A: It was a south paw.

Q: What is the easiest plant to spot in a garden?

A: See-weed.

Q: What do you get when you make a belt entirely out of clocks?

A: A big waist of time.

Q: What do you get when you give your cows everything they want?

A: Spoiled milk.

Q: What do you get when you cross a fish and an elephant?

A: Swim trunks.

Q: What do you call a pebble that is made of paper mache?

A: It's a sham-rock.

Q: What does a proud monkey father call his baby?

A: A chimp off the old block!

Q: What do you get when you cross a cow and a duck?

A: Milk and quackers!

Q: What do you call a snake on a jobsite wearing a hard hat?

A: A boa-constructor.

Q: What do a digital rabbit and a big dog have in common?

A: One is an e-hare and the other is hairy.

Q: How does a spider test-drive a car?

A: He takes it for a spin.

Q: Why did the frankfurter only eat deep-dish pizza?

A: It was a Chicago dog.

Q: Why did the piano player keep banging his head into the piano?

A: He liked playing by ear.

Q: What do you call a sleeping dinosaur?

A: Dino-snore.

Q: Why did the house take its medicine?

A: It had a windowpane.

Q: Why did the cemetery need a fence?

A: People were dying to get in.

Q: What happens when the beach acts mean?

A: The tide goes out and never comes back.

Q: Where do alien cats get their milk?

A: From flying saucers.

Q: What drink do cheerleaders like the most?

A: Root beer.

Q: What fruit does Beethoven like the most?

A: Ba-na-na-na!

Q: What kind of cell phone did Delilah use?

A: Samson.

Q: Did you hear I got fired from the auto shop?

A: They caught me taking a brake!

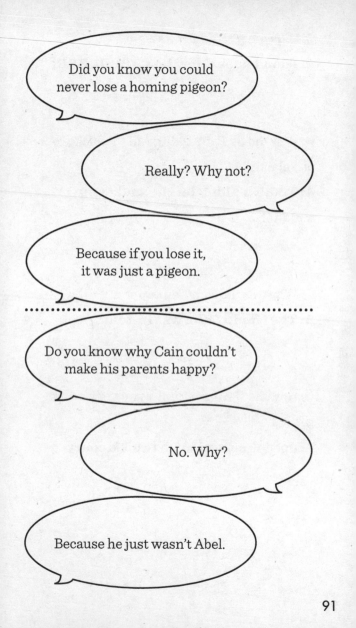

91

Q: Why are pirates always right?

A: I don't know, they just ARRRRRRR!

Q: Why did St. Patrick drive all the snakes out of Ireland?

A: They wouldn't let the snakes on a plane!

Q: Why was the camping trip so stressful?

A: The whole thing was in-tents.

Q: How did the first tennis match of the Bible get started?

A: Joseph served in Pharaoh's court.

Q: Where did the computer hang out?

A: At the mouse pad.

Q: How did the troll get a stomachache?

A: From goblin everything in sight!

Q: What is the best day at the beach?

A: SUNday.

Q: What do you call a pack of bears without ears?

A: A pack of b.

Chicken jokes are some of the most common jokes out there, and people keep making up new ones every day. "Chicken-cross-the-road" jokes are really fun to say in bunches. Start with the classic, and then fire off more to go with it.

Try these four:

Q: Why did the chicken cross the road?

A: To get to the other side.

Q: Why did the chicken cross the playground?

A: To get to the other slide.

Q: Why did the chicken cross the beach?

A: To get to the other tide.

Q: Why did the elephant cross the road?

A: It was the chicken's day off.

Now these four:

Q: Why did the chicken cross the road?

A: To get to the other side.

Q: Why did the hamburger cross the road?

A: It was following the chicken.

Q: Why did the French fries cross the road?

A: They were following the hamburger.

Q: Why didn't the tomato cross the road?

A: It was following the fries, but it couldn't ketchup.

If you're daring, try eight in a row:

Q: Why did the chicken cross the road?

A: To get to the other side.

Q: Why did the chicken cross the road?

A: The road had it coming.

Q: Why did the robot cross the road when it saw a fight?

A: It was programmed by a chicken.

Q: Why did the chicken go up the stairs?

A: She had already crossed the road.

Q: Why did the rooster cross the road?

A: To impress all the chicks.

Q: Why did the skunk cross the road?

A: Because the other side stinks.

Q: Why did the rabbit think he could cross the road?

A: He didn't; he just hopped he could.

Q: Why did the dinosaur cross the road?

A: The chicken wasn't born yet.

Here are some more fun chicken jokes:

Q: How do you grow a vegetarian chicken?

A: With an eggplant.

Q: Why did the chicken get in trouble?

A: For using fowl language.

Q: Why was the chicken arrested?

A: It was suspected of fowl play.

Q: Why was the turkey kicked out of the chicken's baseball game?

A: For hitting too many fowl balls.

Q: Why did the egg hide?

A: It was a little chicken.

Q: How did the chicken get in the band?

A: By bringing drumsticks.

Q: Why did the chicken join the gym?

A: For the eggs-ercise.

Q: Why did Beethoven get rid of all his chickens?

A: They kept screaming, "Bach! Bach! Bach!"

And one really long chicken joke . . .
A chicken strutted into a library and said,
"Book, book, book . . . book, book." The librarian
gave the chicken a book. It took the book and
strutted back out of the library, looking and
feeling quite happy.

HOWEVER, fifteen minutes later, the chicken
showed up again. It didn't look happy. It
dropped the book on the counter, and said,
"Book, book, book." Slightly confused, the
librarian gave the chicken a different book, and
off strutted the chicken.

HOWEVER, fifteen minutes after THAT, the
chicken was back AGAIN. Looking quite upset,
it said, "Book, book, booook!" Fully confused,
the librarian gave the chicken yet another book.

When fifteen minutes later the process
repeated itself AGAIN, the annoyed librarian
gave the chicken another book but this time
decided to follow it. The chicken strutted out
of the library and up the street until it reached
the park. It strutted through the park to a fallen
tree. Sitting on the tree was a frog. The chicken
strutted up to the frog, dropped the book in
front of the frog, and said, "Book, book, book."
The frog took one look at the book and said,
"Read it, read it, read it."

Knock-Knock
Jokes

Knock knock!
Who's there?
Annie.
Annie who?
Annie one you like!

Knock knock!
Who's there?
Al.
Al who?
Al give you a big hug if you open the door!

Knock knock!
Who's there?
Cereal.
Cereal who?
Ce-real pleasure to make your acquaintance!

Knock knock!
Who's there?
Claire.
Claire who?
Claire out of the way! We're coming in!

Knock knock!
Who's there?
Lion.
Lion who?
Lion here waiting for you to open the door!

Knock knock!
Who's there?
Doughnut.
Doughnut who?
Doughnut ask too many details. Just open the door!

Knock knock!
Who's there?
Dwayne.
Dwayne who?
Dwayne the bathtub, I'm dwowning here!

Knock knock!
Who's there?
Eileen.
Eileen who?
Eileen'd on the door knocker by accident.

Knock knock!
Who's there?
Matthew.
Matthew who?
Matthew is untied. Can you help me?

Knock knock!
Who's there?
Mark.
Mark who?
No, Mark where? Mark's here.

Knock knock!
Who's there?
Luke.
Luke who?
Luke, I am not gonna stand out here all day. Can I come in?

Knock knock!
Who's there?
John.
John who?
John to let me in? Or should I just stay out here all day?

Knock knock!
Who's there?
Annie.
Annie who?
Annie one going to open this door already?

Knock knock!
Who's there?
Bee.
Bee who?
Don't worry, bee happy!

Knock knock!
Who's there?
Anita.
Anita who?
Anita borrow a cup of sugar.

Knock knock!
Who's there?
Arthur.
Arthur who?
Arthur any names I can say that will get you to open this door?

Knock knock!
Who's there?
Bach.
Bach who?
Bach, bach. It's the chicken from across the road.

Knock knock!
Who's there?
Banana.
Banana who?
Banana split.

Knock knock!
Who's there?
Barbie Q.
Barbie Q who?
Barbie Q pork sandwich!

Knock knock!
Who's there?
Kanga.
Kanga who?
No silly, it's kangaROO!

Knock knock!
Who's there?
Cain.
Cain who?
Cain I come in?

Knock knock!
Who's there?
Abel.
Abel who?
Are you Abel to open the door or am I supposed to stand out here with Cain?

Knock knock!
Who's there?
Dozen.
Dozen who?
Dozen anybody plan on opening this door? It's cold out here!

Knock knock!
Who's there?
Figs.
Figs who?
Figs your front step—I almost tripped coming to the door!

Knock knock!
Who's there?
Figs.
Figs who?
Figs your doorbell—the thing is not working!

Knock knock!
Who's there?
Figs.
Figs who?
Figs me something to eat, and I'll stop with the knock-knock jokes!

Knock knock!
Who's there?
Frank.
Frank who?
Frank you for asking. It is I!

Knock knock!
Who's there?
Frank.
Frank who?
Frank you for being a friend.

Knock knock!
Who's there?
From.
From who?
Well actually, if we are being grammatically accurate, I believe you mean "from whom?"

Knock knock!
Who's there?
Noah.
Noah who?
I Noah guy that can get that doorbell fixed.

Knock knock!
Who's there?
G.I.
G.I. who?
G.I. don't know.

Knock knock!
Who's there?
G.I.
G.I. who?
G.I. wish you would open up.

Knock knock!
Who's there?
G.I.
G.I. who?
G.I. guess it is whoever is going to get you to open this door!

Knock knock!
Who's there?
Ivana.
Ivana who?
Ivana come in. Would you please open the door?

Knock knock!
Who's there?
Justin.
Justin who?
Justin case you missed it, it's raining. So could we go inside, please?

Knock knock!
Who's there?
Justin.
Justin who?
Justin the neighborhood and thought I'd say hello.

Knock knock!
Who's there?
Jamaican.
Jamaican who?
Jamaican pancakes? I'm starved.

Knock knock!
Who's there?
Jamaican.
Jamaican who?
Jamaican me ask to come in again?

Knock knock!
Who's there?
Jamaican.
Jamaican who?
Jamaican it harder to get in here than I expected.

Knock knock!
Who's there?
Jamaican.
Jamaican who?
**Jamaican me think of too
many jokes!**

Knock knock!
Who's there?
Jamaican.
Jamaican who?
**Jamaican me crazy. Now open
the door!**

Knock knock!
Who's there?
Jamaica.
Jamaica who?
**Jamaica great host. Now please
let me in! And about those
pancakes . . .**

Knock knock!
Who's there?
Ken.
Ken who?
Ken I come in?

Knock knock!
Who's there?
Ken.
Ken who?
Ken you just open the door and see for yourself?

Knock knock!
Who's there?
Kent.
Kent who?
Kent you see it is me?

Knock knock!
Who's there?
Ketchup.
Ketchup who?
Ketchup to me and you will see.

Knock knock!
Who's there?
Kiwi.
Kiwi who?
Kiwi eat now? I'm starving!

Knock knock!
Who's there?
Larva.
Larva who?
I-a larva you! Do you-a larva me too?

Knock knock!
Who's there?
Puss.
Puss who?
**Pussibly the coolest cat
you know!**

Knock knock!
Who's there?
Pooch.
Pooch who?
**Pooch your heads together and
figure it out!**

Knock knock!
Who's there?
Butch.
Butch who?
**Butch your arms around me.
I'm cold.**

Knock knock!
Who's there?
Jimmy.
Jimmy who?
Jimmy a kiss!

Knock knock!
Who's there?
Joe.
Joe who?
Did you want me to Joe home?

Knock knock!
Who's there?
Butch, Jimmy, and Joe.
Butch, Jimmy, and Joe who?
**Butch your arms around me,
Jimmy a kiss, or I'll Joe home!**

Knock knock!
Who's there?
Double.
Double who?
W.

Knock knock!
Who's there?
Ima.
Ima who?
Ima gonna keep knocking until you open this door!

Knock knock!
Who's there?
Wooden shoe.
Wooden shoe?
Wooden shoe like to hear more jokes?

Knock knock!
Who's there?
Just a little girl.
Just a little girl who?
**Just a little girl who can't reach
the doorbell!**

Knock knock!
Who's there?
Abby.
Abby who?
Abby birthday!

Knock knock!
Who's there?
Radio.
Radio who?
Radio or not, I'm comin' in!

Knock knock!
Who's there?
Rita.
Rita who?
Rita KNOCK-KNOCK ROCKS joke book and you might know the answer!

Knock knock!
Who's there?
Wooden shoe.
Wooden shoe who?
Wooden shoe like to know?

Knock knock!
Who's there?
Beef.
Beef who?
Beef-ore it starts raining, do you think you could open the door?

Knock knock!
Who's there?
Ya.
Ya who?
Great, I'm glad you are excited.

Knock knock!
Who's there?
Yacht.
Yacht who?
Yacht to open the door before I tell another joke.

Knock knock!
Who's there?
Yacht.
Yacht who?
Yacht to stop asking if you don't want to know the answer.

Knock knock!
Who's there?
Yacht.
Yacht who?
Yacht to have guessed I can go on and on and on . . .

Knock knock!
Who's there?
Yacht.
Yacht who?
Yacht to know by now I've got more jokes where these came from.

Knock knock!
Who's there?
Yacht.
Yacht who?
Yacht to buy me another KNOCK-KNOCK ROCKS joke book so I can get some new material!